In Conversation
A Writer's Guidebook
with Exercises

Second Edition

MIKE PALMQUIST, *Colorado State University*

BARBARA WALLRAFF

Exercises and content for multilingual writers contributed by
EMILY SUH, *Texas State University*

bedford/st.martin's
Macmillan Learning
Boston | New York

For Bedford/St. Martin's

Vice President, Editorial, Macmillan Learning Humanities: Edwin Hill
Executive Program Director for English: Leasa Burton
Executive Program Manager: Stacey Purviance
Marketing Manager: Vivian Garcia
Director of Content Development, Humanities: Jane Knetzger
Senior Developmental Editor: Rachel Goldberg
Assistant Editor: Aislyn Fredsall
Senior Content Project Manager: Gregory Erb
Senior Workflow Project Manager: Jennifer L. Wetzel
Production Supervisor: Brianna Lester
Senior Media Project Manager: Allison Hart
Senior Media Editor: Barbara G. Flanagan
Composition: Lumina Datamatics, Inc.
Text Permissions Manager: Kalina Ingham
Text Permissions Researcher: Elaine Kosta, Lumina Datamatics, Inc.
Photo Permissions Editor: Angela Boehler
Photo Researcher: Krystyna Borgen, Lumina Datamatics, Inc.
Director of Design, Content Management: Diana Blume
Text Design: Diana Blume and Laura Shaw Design, Inc.
Cover Design: William Boardman
Cover Image: Yippa/Moment/Getty Images
Printing and Binding: King Printing Co., Inc.

Printed in the United States of America

1   2   3   4   5   6   24   23   22   21   20

For information, write:
Bedford/St. Martin's, 75 Arlington Street, Boston, MA 02116

ISBN   978-1-319-36119-8 (Student Edition)
ISBN   978-1-319-36120-4 (Student Edition with Exercises)

Acknowledgments
Acknowledgments and copyrights appear on the same page as the text and art selections they cover; these acknowledgments and copyrights constitute an extension of the copyright page.

How to Use This Book

In Conversation is divided into six color-coded parts, with advice and examples for every stage of the writing process.

1 Part 1, Join the Conversation, helps you recognize yourself as a writer and develop critical thinking skills.

2 Part 2, Work with Genre and Design, introduces you to common types of documents and guides you in composing and designing, whether for a course assignment or on your own.

3 Part 3, Conduct Research, instructs you in how to find, evaluate, and manage your sources and avoid plagiarism.

4 Part 4, Draft Your Document, helps you move from research to a full-fledged draft, with attention to thesis statement, argument and evidence, organization, and synthesizing source materials.

5 Part 5, Revise and Edit, focuses on making your writing stand out, with strategies for writing clearly, correctly, and skillfully.

6 Part 6, Document Sources, explains how to cite your sources correctly in four different documentation systems—MLA, APA, *Chicago*, and CSE—with dozens of model citations and full-page tutorials.

To learn more about a topic, follow the cross-references. These yellow arrows lead you to related information in other parts of the book.

How Can I . . .

- Find a broad topic quickly? See the Brief Contents (inside front cover).
- Look up specific writing, research, or design advice? See the Detailed Contents (inside back cover).
- Learn how to design my document? See the Genre Design Gallery (G) for real-world models, helpful annotations, and handy checklists.
- Resolve a sticky writing problem? See the yellow Writer to Writer boxes for succinct advice on tough situations.

- Learn the difference between "affect" and "effect"? See Frequently Confused, Misused, and Abused Words (p. G-1) to clear up confusion about easily misspelled or misunderstood words.
- Define terms my instructor uses? See the Glossary of Terms (p. G-7) to understand important grammar, writing, research, and design terminology.
- Interpret my instructor's feedback on my essay? See the Common Revision Symbols and Notations (p. C-1) to learn what those marks mean.
- Get advice for multilingual writers? See the Help for Multilingual Writers menu below for topics of special interest to students whose first language is not English.
- View a student model? See the menu of Models and Advice for Student Writing below for examples of other students' work.

Preface

Imagine two writers, one living a few city blocks from the Atlantic Ocean and the other living 2,000 miles away in the Rocky Mountains. Imagine they're collaborating on a complex project, meeting face-to-face only rarely, and coming from very different starting points. Barbara has spent more than three decades as a professional editor, including many years as a senior editor at *The Atlantic*, while Mike has worked almost equally long as a college professor and before that as a professional writer.

Given our backgrounds, we haven't agreed on every aspect of writing and researching, or on every point of style. We certainly don't agree on how to write the possessives of proper nouns ending in "s." And that's fine. We both recognize that respectable opinion varies about plenty of things related to writing. In fact, many of the "Writer to Writer" discussions in this book grew out of our disagreements.

Fortunately, we agree on the important issues. From the start, we agreed that this book should be brief yet comprehensive; that it should approach writing from a rhetorical perspective; and that, despite its brevity, it should not sacrifice the details and examples that can help writers find their way through their most critical writing challenges. We also agreed to avoid the typical teacher-to-student stance used so often in textbooks. Instead, we've approached this book as experienced writers seeking to share what we've learned with other writers.

We recognize, of course, that many readers will not think of themselves as writers. We'd point out, though, that they write frequently: on social media, in email and text messages, for school publications, for personal blogs or journals. Our goal is to help our readers draw on their experiences with writing—and with conversation more generally—to write clearly, effectively, and compellingly.

This book, *In Conversation*, is the result. Practical and highly visual, it answers the questions that come up throughout our writing and research processes. This second edition offers more coverage for multilingual writers, new real-world examples, and stronger attention to authenticating sources. Here's hoping that you—like the many instructors and colleagues who have given us helpful feedback—find it a valuable guide to writing in the twenty-first century.

New to this Edition

- ⊕ **New content for multilingual writers.** New sections throughout

> **27.5** Use Articles Artfully ⊕
>
> The words *a*, *an*, and *the* are **articles**. (The term comes from the Latin *articulus*, meaning "part," or in this case, specifically a "small connecting part.") *A* and *an* are called **indefinite articles**,

Part 5 support students whose first language is not English. Look for this icon to find all of our new coverage, from count versus noncount nouns and phrasal verbs to question word order and common spelling rules.

- **A version with exercises, for more student practice.** *In Conversation 2e with Exercises* contains 55 sets of exercises on common style, grammar, punctuation, and mechanics issues. Answers to odd-numbered questions in the back of the book give students a chance to self-check.

- **Critical attention to evaluating and authenticating sources in the era of "fake news."** A revised Chapter 7 arms students with the tools to assess bias, pop information bubbles, and seek alternative points of view.

- **More coverage of analysis.** A reorganized Chapter 12, Support Your Main Point, addresses analytical writing as well as argumentative writing, with specific information on causal analysis, data analysis, and trend analysis.

Features of the Book

- **A framework of writing as conversation, emphasizing the rhetorical situation, genre, and design.** *In Conversation* grounds writers in a deep understanding of their purpose, audience, and context. This emphasis has shaped the examples we use, the issues we highlight in our "Writer to Writer" features, and the genres and design strategies we discuss, particularly in the Genre Design Gallery in Part 2.

- **A Writer to Writer approach.** More than 45 conversational "Writer to Writer" boxes help writers gain a nuanced understanding of issues ranging from context to composing processes to points of disagreement about style, grammar, and mechanics. Talking *as* writers *to* writers, we use these brief boxes to offer advice and answer questions such as "Is it okay to use contractions?" or "Help! How can I write a paper under pressure?"

  Writer to Writer

  Can you use an essay in more than one class? Reusing an assignment for more than one class, often referred to as self-plagiarism, is generally frowned on by writing instructors. If you wrote a term paper in one class and then turned it in for a grade in another, you wouldn't learn anything new about conducting research, developing an argument, considering your readers, and so on.

  On the other hand, if you've written previously about a topic that still intrigues you, you might ask your instructor if you could build on your earlier work. Similarly, if you're working on a new topic that is relevant to two of your current classes, you might talk with your instructors about completing a more ambitious project for both classes.

- **A striking visual approach that pays special attention to genre and design.** Taking a cue from the vibrant world of social media, our eye-catching visual approach features annotated models from various genres, from traditional academic essays to multimodal essays, infographics to articles. The **Genre Design Gallery** showcases real student writing and published work from a variety of disciplines.

- **Practical attention to the genres students compose in, especially argument.** Chapter 4, Choose Your Genre, gives writers the tools to work in a variety of genres, both inside the classroom and out. The Genre Design Gallery guides them in fashioning a variety of documents that communicate their points clearly and effectively.

- **Comprehensive coverage of information literacy.** Part 3 presents strategies for identifying, locating, and working with sources. We've paid a great deal of attention to how writers can acknowledge what others have written and create a space for their own contributions. We also discuss tools writers can use to produce effective, well-designed, accessible documents. We frame our discussions of working with information technologies not as a set of mechanical processes but as a set of choices shaped by rhetorical situation.

- **Attention to writing across disciplines, professions, and civic and political settings.** Because we hope that this book will be useful throughout a writer's life, we've included genres used in typical first-year writing courses and beyond to prepare students for their writing lives in the professional world.

- **A clear and conversational treatment of grammar, mechanics, and style.** Rather than presenting grammar and style as a set of hard-and-fast rules, Part 5 offers an accessible, thoughtful approach to issues that often vex writers. Annotated, student-friendly examples help students understand *why* grammar, style, and punctuation conventions have developed the way they have and what effects they have on an audience.

- **Practical tips on managing writing projects and information from sources.** Managing writing projects and organizing information from sources are especially difficult for writers who are just beginning to take on complex writing tasks as college students. Throughout *In Conversation*, we call attention to strategies writers can use to stay focused and keep track of information.

Besides sharing practical strategies to help with every stage of the writing process—from generating good ideas to polishing a final draft—this book also demonstrates how those strategies turn out. *In Conversation* is a clear, well-written guide to writing clearly and well. We hope you find it as enjoyable to read as we found it to write.

MIKE PALMQUIST, Colorado State University

BARBARA WALLRAFF, Independent Writing and Editing Professional

Acknowledgments

We are grateful to the many instructors who reviewed *In Conversation* during its development and shared their experience, ideas, and feedback with us:

Angelina Blank, SUNY Potsdam; Cheryl Caesar, Michigan State University; Polina Chemishanova, University of North Carolina at Pembroke; Daniel Compora, University of Toledo; Darren DeFrain, Wichita State University; Tom Deromedi, Mott Community College; Joshua Dickinson, Jefferson Community College; Regina Dilgen, Palm Beach State College–Lakeworth; Mike DuBose, University of Toledo; Jessica Enoch, University of Maryland; Jacqueline Goffe-McNish, Dutchess Community College; George Grella, University of Rochester; Joel Henderson, Chattanooga State Community College; Kristin Iacopelli, University of Toledo; Whitney Jacobson, University of Minnesota Duluth; Lisa Johnson, Casper College; Elaine Jolayemi, Ivy Tech Community College; Renee Krusemark, Northeast Community College; Rich Lane, Clarion University; Patrick Lewis, California State University, Northridge; Bronwen Llewellyn, Daytona State College; Elizabeth Long, College of Western Idaho; Leslie Lovenstein, University of Arkansas–Pulaski Technical College; Julia Mandel, Kent State University; Matt Messer, Tufts University; Tracy Ann Morse, East Carolina University; Van Piercy, Lone Star College–Tomball; Wanda Pothier-Hill, North Shore Community College; Jacob Ray, University of Toledo; Nancy Risch, Caldwell Community College and Technical Institute; Amy Schmidt, Delta College; Mary Ann Simmons, James Sprunt Community College; Daniel Stanford, Pitt Community College; Benjamin Steingass, University of Toledo; Steffanie Triller Fry, Purdue University Northwest; Jayne Waterman, Ashland University; Kathryn Winograd, Arapahoe Community College; Courtney Wright-Werner, Monmouth University; Savannah Xaver, University of Toledo.

In Conversation also benefited from the dedication and hard work of our Bedford/St. Martin's colleagues. Leasa Burton planted the seed of this book and of this partnership; her steady advocacy has been invaluable. Thank you to Edwin Hill, for continuing

Bedford's commitment to the discipline of composition; Stacey Purviance, for her energetic and capable leadership of the handbook team; Rachel Goldberg, for her always excellent editorial guidance and thoughtful collaboration; Gregory Erb, for his unflappable work as production editor; copyeditor Daniel Nighting, for his attention to detail; and marketing manager Vivian Garcia, for her enthusiastic support.

We are thankful to the many colleagues from the academic and publishing worlds who shared feedback as we worked on this book, particularly Nick Carbone, Sue Doe, Chris Neuwirth, and Richard Young. Special thanks to Emily Suh for ensuring that the book addresses the needs of multilingual writers and for drafting the exercises in *In Conversation with Exercises*. We also thank the many writers we've worked with in the classroom and in the workplace for their inspiration. We thank William Whitworth, who has also inspired us with his superb taste and love of good writing. Finally and most importantly, we thank our families—Jessica, Ellen, Reid, and Jim—for their constant support as we've worked on this book. Without their generosity, this book would not exist.

Bedford/St. Martin's puts you first.

From day one, our goal has been simple: to provide inspiring resources that are grounded in best practices for teaching reading and writing. For more than 35 years, Bedford/St. Martin's has partnered with the field, listening to teachers, scholars, and students about the support writers need. We are committed to helping every writing instructor make the most of our resources.

How can we help *you*?

- Our editors can align our resources to your outcomes through correlation and transition guides for your syllabus. Just ask us.

- Our sales representatives specialize in helping you find the right materials to support your course goals.

- Our Bits blog on the Bedford/St. Martin's English Community (community.macmillan.com) publishes fresh teaching ideas weekly. You'll also find easily downloadable professional resources and links to author webinars on our community site.

Contact your Bedford/St. Martin's sales representative or visit **macmillanlearning.com** to learn more.

Print and Digital Options for *In Conversation*

Choose the format that works best for your course, and ask about our packaging options that offer savings for students.

Print

- **Spiral-bound**   To order the spiral-bound edition, use ISBN 978-1-319-36119-8.

- *In Conversation 2e with Exercises*   To order the version with 55 exercises on grammar, style, punctuation, and mechanics, use ISBN 978-1-319-36120-4.

- *A Student's Companion to In Conversation*   To order the supplement for Accelerated Learning Programs, use ISBN 978-1-319-33078-1.

Digital

- *Innovative digital learning space*   Bedford/St. Martin's suite of digital tools makes it easy to get everyone on the same page by putting student writers at the center. For details, visit **macmillanlearning.com/englishdigital**.

- *Popular e-book formats*   For details about our e-book partners, visit **macmillanlearning.com/ebooks**.

- *Inclusive access*   Enable every student to receive their course materials through your LMS on the first day of class. Macmillan Learning's Inclusive Access program is the easiest, most affordable way to ensure all students have access to quality educational resources. Find out more at **macmillanlearning.com/inclusiveaccess**.

Your Course, Your Way

No two writing programs or classrooms are exactly alike. Our Curriculum Solutions team works with you to design custom options that provide the resources your students need. (Options below require enrollment minimums.)

- *ForeWords for English*   Customize any print resource to fit the focus of your course or program by choosing from a range of prepared topics, such as Sentence Guides for Academic Writers.

- *Macmillan Author Program (MAP)*   Add excerpts or package acclaimed works from Macmillan's trade imprints to connect students with prominent authors and public conversations. A list of popular examples or academic themes is available upon request.

- *Bedford Select*   Build your own print handbook or anthology from a database of more than 800 selections, and add your own materials to create your ideal text. Package with any Bedford/St. Martin's text for additional savings. Visit **macmillanlearning.com/bedfordselect**.

Instructor Resources

You have a lot to do in your course. We want to make it easy for you to find the support you need—and to get it quickly.

Teaching with **In Conversation** is available as a PDF that can be downloaded from **macmillanlearning.com**. In addition to chapter overviews and teaching tips, the instructor's manual includes sample syllabi, correlations to the Council of Writing Program Administrators' Outcomes Statement, and classroom activities.

Part 1

Join the Conversation

Part 1: Join the Conversation

Too many of us think that writing well requires a special set of skills and abilities. In fact, almost anyone can learn to write clearly and effectively with a moderate amount of effort. In this guidebook, you'll learn how to become a confident, effective writer by building on your already extensive understanding of how conversations work.

1. Understand Yourself as a Writer
2. Explore Conversations
3. Read Critically and Actively

01. Understand Yourself as a Writer

What does it mean to be a writer? In movies and books, writers are often portrayed as solitary souls, perhaps a bit prickly (if they write novels or short stories), possibly thoughtful and sensitive (if they write poetry), or even just a bit odd. Writers working as journalists are often shown in a passionate exchange with a colleague or an editor — probably on deadline and feeling pressure to meet it.

Most writers, of course, don't fit these stereotypes. Writers are normal, everyday people. In fact, most people you'll see today *Everything* will be, at some point, writers. They'll post something to Face- *makes* book, Twitter, or Tumblr. They'll email a friend. They'll write a *you a* report for a class. They'll send a text message. They'll submit a *writer* proposal for a project. They'll write in a journal. They'll comment on an article or blog.

In short, they'll use writing to connect with others. Through writing, they'll engage in conversation about issues they care about. They'll use writing to share information and ideas or to advance an argument.

This book treats writing as an extension of the kinds of conversations we engage in on a daily basis. As you use this book, reflect on what you're likely to do, say, and hear in a typical conversation. More often than not, you'll find that the knowledge and skills you've developed through years of spoken conversation will help you communicate with others through writing.

1.1 Think of Writing as a Conversation

Imagine yourself at a party. When you arrived, you said hello to friends and found something to eat or drink. Then you walked around, listening briefly to several conversations. Eventually, you joined a group that was talking about something you found interesting.

If you're like most people, you didn't jump right into the conversation. Instead, you listened for a few minutes and thought about what was being said. Perhaps you learned something new. Eventually, you added your voice to the conversation, other members of the group picked up on what you said, and the conversation moved along.

1.1

Use Your Conversational Skills

Understanding how conversations work can help you become a better writer. Good writing, like good conversation, involves more than simply stating what you know. As writing scholars, notably rhetorician Kenneth Burke, have long argued, writing is a process that involves several activities:

convos & writing go together

- **Careful listening.** Reading critically is a key part of the writing process (see Chapter 3). It involves paying attention both to voices that seem familiar and comfortable and to those that seem unfamiliar, that challenge your understanding and perceptions, and that share ideas in surprising or unusual ways. *be open-minded*

- **Reflection.** Just as you would listen politely and receptively in a face-to-face conversation to someone you've met for the first time, even if they speak in a way that you find new or even surprising, you'll want to reflect on the new ideas they present. You can learn more about writing to reflect on page 39, Sec. 4.1. *think about what was said*

- **Exploration and discovery.** Writing is a process that builds on your reading and reflection in ways that prepare you to add your voice to the conversation.

- **A desire to share your ideas.** Your voice is important. Your perspective is worth sharing. Writing that emerges from thoughtful reflection and inquiry can help others advance their own thinking about an issue you've been exploring. *your writing is important*

You already possess many of the skills that make for a good conversation, and you can use those skills in your writing. You can consider why you're interested in the conversation and why others are, too. And you can explore the contexts—physical, social, and cultural—that will shape how your document is written and read.

Today, many of us are as likely to engage in conversations through writing as through speaking. Some of us prefer a text message to a phone call. Some of us find email far more useful than meetings. And some of us keep up with friends through Facebook, Twitter, or Instagram more than we do in person.

You may not think of creating text messages, email messages, and social media posts as writing, yet it is. And the writing you've done in these settings can help prepare you for the writing you'll be asked to do in class or on the job.

1.1

Add Your Voice

Just as most people listen to what's being said before speaking up, most writers begin the process of writing about a topic by reading. Developing your contribution to a written conversation involves reading critically, reflecting on what you've learned, deciding what and how you want to contribute to the

recic l to start off your writing

Draft your contribution and share it with other members of the conversation.

Begin by reading about a topic or issue, just as you'd listen for a while before speaking.

Look for something new to share with the other participants in the conversation.

Think carefully about what you've read, just as you'd think carefully about what you'd just heard.

Writing is a form of conversation in which readers and writers share ideas about a topic or issue.

conversation, and drafting and sharing your contribution. In turn, others will read and respond to what you've written.

You can see this circular process of exchanges among readers and writers in a number of contexts. Articles in scholarly and professional journals almost always refer to previously published work. Letters to the editor in newspapers and magazines frequently mention earlier letters or articles. Comments on blog posts or tweets that respond to other tweets follow a similar pattern.

1.2 Understand Your Writing Situation

When people participate in a spoken conversation, they pay attention to factors such as why they've joined the conversation, who's involved in the conversation, and what's already been said. They also notice the mood of the people they're speaking with, their facial expressions and body language, and physical factors such as background noise. In short, they consider the situation as they listen and speak. Similarly, when writers engage in written conversation, they become part of a **writing situation**—the setting in which writers and readers communicate with one another.

The phrase *writing situation* is another name for *rhetorical situation*, a concept that has been studied for thousands of years. Viewing writing as a rhetorical act helps us understand how writers or speakers pursue their purposes; consider the needs and interests of their audiences; draw on sources; adapt to the conditions in which they address their audiences; and present, organize, or design their documents or speeches.

What you write about depends on your writing situation—your purposes, readers, sources, and context. In many cases, a writing assignment will identify or suggest these elements for you. If it doesn't, take some time to think about the situation that will shape your work.

Define Your Purposes and Roles

Writers join written conversations for particular **purposes**: to inform, to analyze, to convince or persuade, to solve a problem, and so on. In many cases, writers have more than one purpose,

why?

such as learning something about a subject while earning a good grade or a promotion.

To accomplish their purposes, writers adopt **roles** within a conversation. A writer might explain something to someone else, in a sense becoming a guide through the conversation. Another writer might advance an argument, taking on the role of an

1.2

Writing Purposes and Roles

Purpose	Role	Action
To share reflections on an individual, event, object, idea, or issue	Observer	Consider a topic by sharing what is learned through the process of reflecting on it.
To help readers become aware of the facts and ideas central to an issue	Reporter	Present information on an issue without adopting an argumentative or evaluative position.
To analyze and explain the origins, qualities, significance, or potential impact of an idea, event, or issue	Interpreter	Apply an interpretive framework to a subject and seek answers to an interpretive question.
To assess and help readers reach an informed, well-reasoned understanding of a subject's worth or effectiveness	Evaluator	Make judgments about an individual, event, object, or idea.
To make progress on understanding and developing a solution to a problem	Problem Solver	Identify and define a problem, discuss the effects of a problem, assess potential solutions, and offer a solution.
To convince, persuade, or mediate a dispute among readers	Advocate	Convince readers that a position on an issue is reasonable and well founded, persuade readers to take action, or mediate by bringing readers into agreement on how to address an issue.
To share new knowledge	Inquirer	Conduct research and other forms of inquiry.
To amuse readers	Entertainer	Write in an entertaining way in an attempt to maintain readers' interest (seldom a primary goal of academic or professional writing).

advocate for a particular approach to an issue. As in spoken conversations, these roles are not mutually exclusive. For example, a writer might create a website that both *informs* readers about the potential benefits of geothermal power and *argues* for increased reliance on this form of power.

Your purposes and roles will be shaped by your interests, experiences, knowledge, attitudes, values, and beliefs about the conversation.

Consider Your Readers

Just as writers have purposes, so do readers. Readers often want to learn about a subject, assess or evaluate ideas and arguments, or understand opposing perspectives. And like writers, readers are strongly affected by their own needs, interests, knowledge, experiences, values, and beliefs.

Your assignment might identify your readers, or audience, for you. If you are working on a project for a class, one of your most important readers will be your instructor. Other readers might include your classmates, people who have a professional or personal interest in your topic, or, if your project will be published, the readers of a newspaper, magazine, or website. If you are writing in a business or professional setting, your readers might include supervisors, coworkers, or customers.

Analyze Your Context

Writing is affected by a wide variety of contexts, including social, physical, technological, disciplinary, professional, cultural, and historical contexts.

- **Social contexts** shape the relationships between writers and readers. Are they friends? Strangers? Supervisor and employee? Instructor and student? Whatever the dynamic, social context will influence how writers and readers approach the writing situation. *how will they connect*

- **Physical and technological contexts** affect both the kind of document you choose and the design of your document. *appearance*

Where will you write? What writing tools will you use? Will your document be read in a quiet room, on a train, or in a coffee shop? Will your readers view it in print, on a tablet or phone, or on a large computer screen?

how? will it get done

1.2

- **Disciplinary and professional contexts** are the shared experiences of members of particular disciplines, such as chemistry or sociology. Over time, members of a discipline develop consensus about how to report new findings, how to offer criticism of previous work in the field, and how to document sources.

- **Cultural and historical contexts** are a set of broader similarities and differences among writers and readers. The attack on the World Trade Center on September 11, 2001, is one example of a historical event that has strongly influenced much that has been written about terrorism in the popular press, in professional journals, and on the web. Similarly, widely shared cultural values—such as a belief in the importance of personal freedom—can shape writers' and readers' responses to arguments that support or run counter to those values.

Assess Potential Sources

In spoken conversations, speakers build on what has been said, often referring to specific ideas or arguments and identifying the speakers who raised them. Written conversations also build on earlier contributions. Writers refer to *sources*—or the work of other authors—to support their arguments, provide a context for their own contributions, or differentiate their ideas from those advanced by other authors. Writers also use sources to introduce new ideas, information, and arguments to a conversation. When writers refer to sources, they provide citations to indicate where the information comes from and to help readers locate the sources should they wish to review them.

As you analyze an assignment, determine whether you'll need to draw on information from sources such as magazine or journal articles, websites, or scholarly books. Ask whether you'll need to cite a certain number of sources and whether you're required to use a specific documentation system, such as the system created by the Modern Language Association (MLA) or the American Psychological Association (APA).

1.3

You can read more about finding and using sources in Part 3 of this book.

Consider Genre and Design

Writers make choices about the type of document and the design of their documents largely in response to physical, social, and disciplinary contexts. They recognize that they are more likely to accomplish their purposes if their documents meet their readers' expectations, are designed to help readers understand ideas and information, and present their points clearly and effectively.

Genres are general categories of documents, such as opinion columns, scholarly articles, novels, and blogs. Genres typically develop to help writers accomplish a general purpose—such as informing readers or presenting an argument—within a specific context and for a certain audience. As the needs and interests of a community change, the genres used within that community evolve to reflect those needs and interests.

Document design is closely related to genre. In fact, the characteristic design of a particular type of document, such as the use of columns, headings, and photographs in a magazine article, can help you distinguish one type of document from another. Throughout this book, you'll find design treated as a central writing strategy.

You can find in-depth discussions of genre and design in Part 2.

1.3 Manage Your Writing Processes

Writing is a lot like skiing. It's also a lot like teaching, coaching, managing a budget, and selling trucks. In fact, there are surprising similarities among these and other complex activities. The

EasyWriter

2020 APA Update

Andrea A. Lunsford

Brief Contents

Quick Start Menu

Find your assignment, and then start with the advice and examples listed here.
✳ indicates content in *LaunchPad Solo for Lunsford Handbooks*. (See the outside back cover flap for details.)

Don't see your project listed here?
- See a complete list of chapters on the inside front cover (Brief Contents).
- See a detailed list of sections on the inside back cover (Detailed Contents).
- Search an alphabetical list of topics and terms on pages 365–96 (Index/Glossary).
- Find more examples of student writing in *LaunchPad Solo for Lunsford Handbooks*.

What Are You Writing?	Get Advice	See Student Models
Abstract	**7c** Summarizing **16b** Following APA manuscript format	**16e** Causal analysis with abstract
Annotated bibliography	**12** Evaluating Sources and Taking Notes (in particular **12g**, Creating an annotated bibliography)	**12h** Annotated bibliography entries ✳ Annotated bibliography (Tony Chan) ✳ Reflective annotated bibliography (Nandita Sriram)
Argument	**8** Arguing Ethically and Persuasively	**8g** Argument essay
Blog	**Checklist:** Participating in Class Blogs, Wikis, and Other Forums (p. 41) **9d** Choosing genres for public writing	✳ Reflective blog post (Thanh Nguyen)
Film analysis	**7d** Analyzing **8e** Making an argument	✳ Film analysis (Amrit Rao)
Job application	**1f** Considering audiences **3b** Appropriate formats **8e** Making an argument	✳ Cover letter (Nastassia Lopez) ✳ Résumés (Megan Lange)
Lab report	**9a** Recognizing expectations of academic disciplines **9c** Adapting genre structures	✳ Lab report in chemistry (Allyson Goldberg)
Literary analysis	**7** Reading and Listening Analytically, Critically, and Respectfully **15** MLA Style	**9e** Excerpts from a close reading of poetry ✳ Close reading of poetry (Bonnie Sillay)

What Are You Writing?	Get Advice	See Student Models
Multimodal project	**3** Making Design Decisions **9** Writing in a Variety of Disciplines and Genres	**9e** Samples in a variety of disciplines and genres [Poster, Fundraising web page, Web comic, Newsletter] ✳ Pitch package (Deborah Jane and Jamie Burke)
Personal reflection	**5c** Reflecting on your own work	**5d** Reflection ✳ Portfolio cover letter (James Kung)
Portfolio	**3** Making Design Decisions **5b** Creating a portfolio	**5d** Reflection ✳ Portfolio cover letter (James Kung)
Poster	**3c** Visuals and media **3d** Ethical use of visuals and media **9d** Choosing genres for public writing	**9e** Samples in a variety of disciplines and genres [Poster]
Presentation	**10** Creating Presentations	**10h** Excerpts from a presentation ✳ Presentation (Shuqiao Song)
Proposal	**8** Arguing Ethically and Persuasively	✳ Pitch package (Deborah Jane and Jamie Burke) ✳ Research proposal (Tara Gupta)
Research project	**Research** (p. 81) **15** MLA Style (literature or languages) **16** APA Style (social sciences) **17** *Chicago* Style (history or the arts) **18** CSE Style (sciences)	**15f** Research-based argument, MLA style **16e** Causal analysis essay with abstract, APA style **17d** Research-based history essay (excerpts), *Chicago* style **18d** Biology literature review (excerpts), CSE style ✳ Complete papers in history and science
Rhetorical analysis	**7c** Summarizing **7d** Analyzing **8e** Making an argument	**7e** Rhetorical analysis
Social media and websites	**1b** Moving between informal and formal writing **1c** Email and other "in-between" writing **3** Making Design Decisions **9d** Choosing genres for public writing	**1b** Moving between informal and formal writing [Student tweets] **9e** Samples in a variety of disciplines and genres [Fundraising web page, Web comic]
Summary	**7c** Summarizing	✳ Summary of an assigned reading (Sarah Lum)
Visuals	**3c** Visuals and media **3d** Ethical use of visuals and media	**9e** Samples in a variety of disciplines and genres [Poster, Fundraising web page, Web comic, Newsletter]